The **Platypus**

by Pauline Reilly

W9-AOJ-314

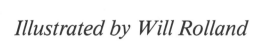

Illustrated by Will Rolland

Kangaroo Press

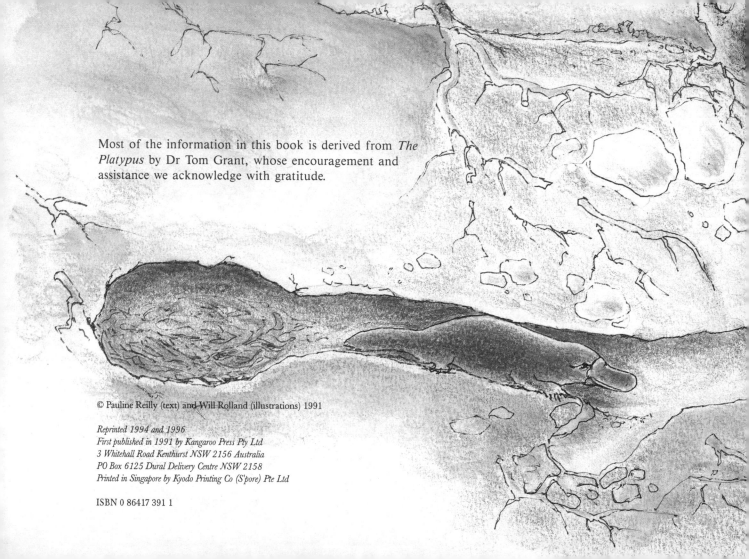

Most of the information in this book is derived from *The Platypus* by Dr Tom Grant, whose encouragement and assistance we acknowledge with gratitude.

© Pauline Reilly (text) and Will Rolland (illustrations) 1991

Reprinted 1994 and 1996
First published in 1991 by Kangaroo Press Pty Ltd
3 Whitehall Road Kenthurst NSW 2156 Australia
PO Box 6125 Dural Delivery Centre NSW 2158
Printed in Singapore by Kyodo Printing Co (S'pore) Pte Ltd

ISBN 0 86417 391 1

In late summer,
when Platypus was nearly four months old,
she followed her brother along the tunnel
from the nest where the air was stuffy and stale.

Her mother followed behind.

3

At the tunnel entrance,
the young platypuses breathed fresh air
for the first time.

Then they slithered into the water
and splashed and played together.

They swam with their front feet,
one foot after the other, while their back feet
trailed behind only to steer them.
Their front feet were like paddles.

On the swimming stroke, a big flap
of skin underneath the toes opened up.

On the return stroke, the flap folded back
and their feet cut easily through the water.

Each time they dived, they closed their eyes
and ears and nostrils, staying underwater
for a minute or more.

On the bottom of the stream,
they swung their bills from side to side,
turning over sand and little stones.
Insect larvae and other grubs
gave out tiny electrical pulses, or waves,
that reached their sensitive bills.

6

The platypuses grasped the larvae
in their bills and stowed
them in their cheek pouches.
On the surface, they chewed up the larvae
with the horny pads inside their mouths.

After Platypus and her brother had fed,
they returned to the nest with their mother.
They still drank her milk, though they were
not much smaller than she was.

8

Even when it was hot during the day,
the platypuses were cool in their burrow.

9

Early in the autumn, the young platypuses no longer needed
their mother's care. They swam away from the pool
but did not stay together.

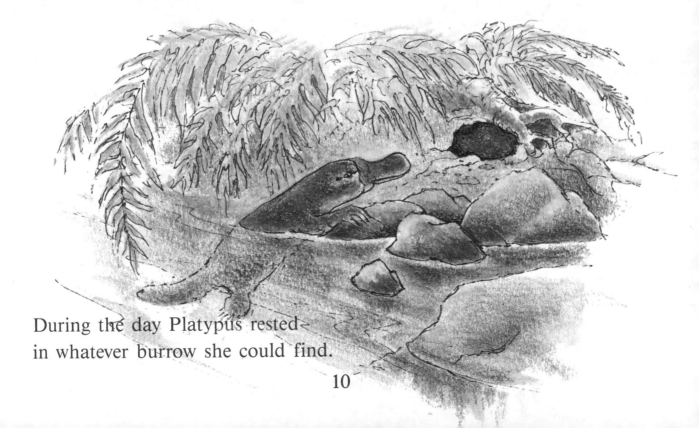

During the day Platypus rested
in whatever burrow she could find.

In the middle of winter,
ice settled on the surface of the water
where the stream ran slowly,
but Platypus continued to feed.

Platypus was not cold. Two layers of thick fur
trapped warm air next to her skin.
Her temperature remained at a steady level
though it was lower than that of other mammals,
including humans.

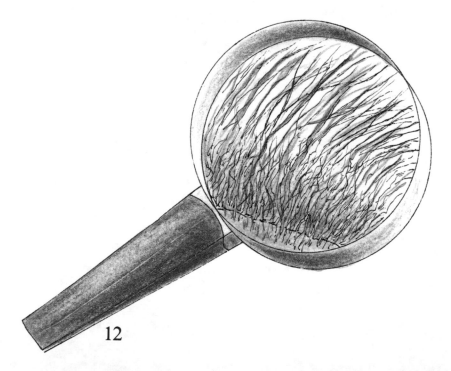

When a big eel swam up to her,
Platypus left the water quickly
and dived into a burrow.

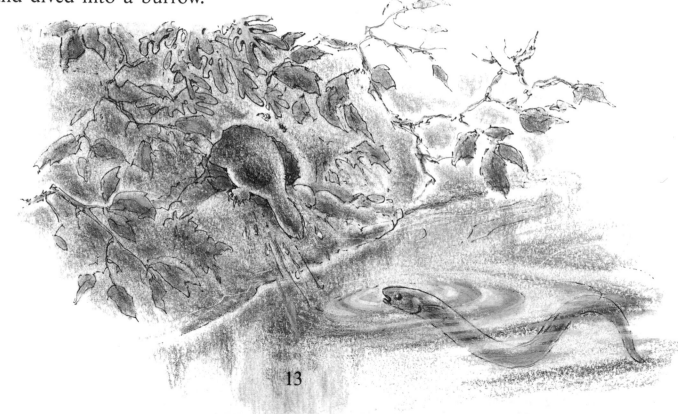

Another time, she swam into a fisherman's net,
even though fishing with nets was not allowed by law.
She thrashed about, trying to reach the surface to breathe.

The fisherman, thinking he had caught a big fish,
jumped into the water and lifted her out.

Then he slipped and Platypus wriggled free.

14

Platypus had a little spur on each of her back legs.
This spur fell off at the end of winter
but Platypus noticed that the spurs on the young males
had grown much bigger than hers had ever been.

15

When snow in the highlands melted,
the stream became a roaring torrent.

The older platypuses knew how to manage in the torrent

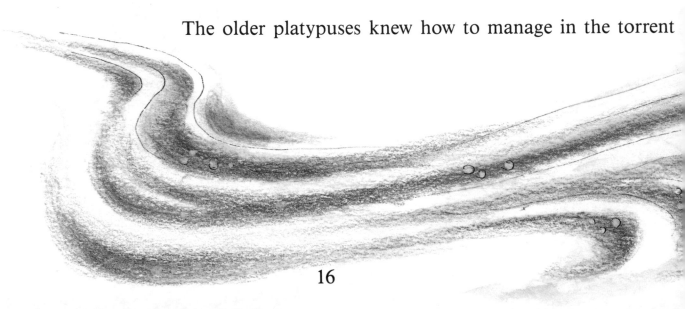

16

but Platypus was swept away downstream
until the waters spread across a floodplain and became quieter.

Soon water on the floodplain
began to dry up into separate pools.

Platypus tried to find her way back to the river.

She travelled from one pool to the next,
but all were shrinking until they were
too shallow for swimming.

18

When a Marsh Harrier flew low overhead,
Platypus hid behind some reeds.

She lay just below the surface, with only her nostrils
above water to let her breathe. She was hungry.
All the fat stored in her tail had gone
and it was thin, like a strap.

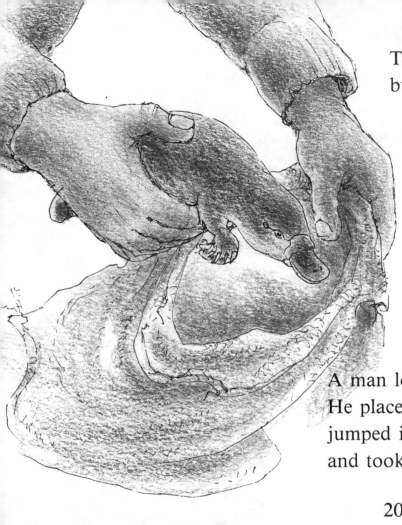

The water in the pool was too warm
but there were no burrows
    where Platypus could keep cool.

She splashed about in distress
    in her useless search
        for food and shelter.

A man looking for frogs saw her splashes.
He placed her gently in a bag,
jumped into his car
and took her back to the big river.

20

Platypus dived into the fresh cool water.
She ate, and ate, and ate.

21

Next spring, when Platypus was two years old,
she was ready to mate.

She dug a nesting burrow, not like
the little ones she had used for resting.

Rocks or roots of trees made her change direction
but soon her burrow was long and safe
and just wide enough for her.

She watched two males fighting.
One of them was stronger.

He dug his spurs into
the other platypus
and sent him away from the pool.

23

Platypus swam round close to the male.
He took her tail in his bill, they circled round the pool
and they mated in the water.

Platypus collected nesting material
of grass and weeds in her bill
and built a nest at the end of the tunnel.

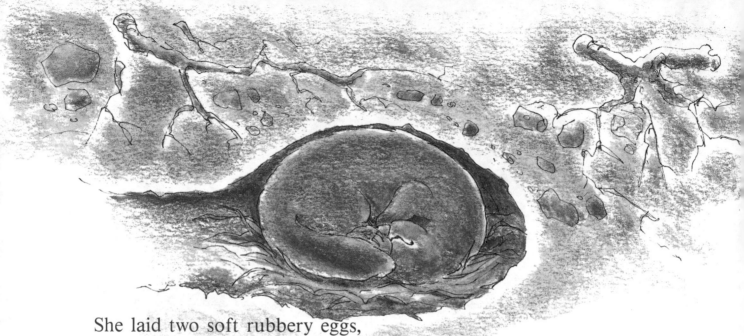

She laid two soft rubbery eggs,
each about the size of a small grape,
and curled her tail and body round them to keep them warm.
For more than a week, she incubated them
all day and all night until they hatched.

Each tiny platypus baby cut its way
out of the soft shell, using the egg tooth on the tip of its bill,
and crawled to one of the two milk patches on its mother's belly.

Platypus spent most of the time
in the nest with her babies.
She gave them very rich milk and they grew fast.

When she went to feed herself in the stream,
she left plugs of earth along the tunnel
so that nothing could find her babies.

28

When the babies were nearly four months old,
just as their mother had done before them,
they crawled out of the burrow,

    slithered into the water,
      played together
        and learned to feed themselves.

Platypus would not breed every year,
especially in those years when there was
a drought, or a flood and not enough food.

29

Scientists were astonished when they first examined a platypus.
It was not like any other living animal.

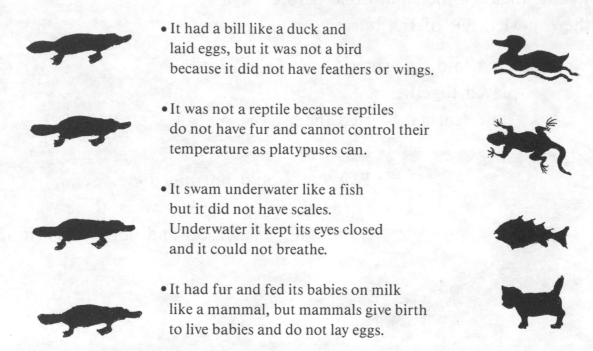

- It had a bill like a duck and
laid eggs, but it was not a bird
because it did not have feathers or wings.

- It was not a reptile because reptiles
do not have fur and cannot control their
temperature as platypuses can.

- It swam underwater like a fish
but it did not have scales.
Underwater it kept its eyes closed
and it could not breathe.

- It had fur and fed its babies on milk
like a mammal, but mammals give birth
to live babies and do not lay eggs.

It *is* a mammal, but a special kind called a Monotreme.
That means, it has one opening for passing droppings and laying eggs.

The scientific name of the platypus
is *Ornithorhynchus anatinus* (Ornith-or-rink-́us anna-tine-́us).
Ornithorhynchus means birdlike snout and *anatinus* means ducklike.

The platypus is most closely related to the echidna,
which also lays eggs and suckles its young.
Platypuses and echidnas are more closely related
to each other than to any other living mammal.

The adult male platypus is one of the few poisonous mammals
in the world and the only one in Australia.
The venom in its spurs can cause great pain to humans.

Platypuses are known to have lived
for more than 12 years in the wild
and for more than 20 years in captivity.

Platypuses live all along the eastern part of Australia.
There are many platypuses in our freshwater streams and lakes
where the water is not polluted.

Sit still and silently on the bank of a stream
at dusk or dawn.
Then you may see a platypus
slithering down the bank and diving into the water.
Watch for the ripples on the surface
when it comes up for air.